The Stations
of the Cross
for Children

A Dramatized Presentation

Rita Coleman

A Liturgical Press Book

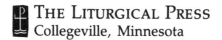

THE LITURGICAL PRESS
Collegeville, Minnesota

First edition 1991
THE COLUMBA PRESS
County Dublin, Ireland

Design and illustration by Bill Bolger

*For my parents
Vincent and Kathleen*

ISBN 0-8146-2062-0

INTRODUCTION

Fr Brendan O'Reilly, a priest in Beaumont Parish, Dublin, where I teach, invited me to compile a script to dramatise the Stations of the Cross for Children. My class of seven- and eight-year-olds would enact the story in the Parish Church on Good Friday.

On Good Friday most churches provide a Remembrance Service of the crucifixion day. However, these services very often fail to capture the interest and attention of the children. Young people need direct images with which they can identify.

To overcome this problem, I wanted to portray the crucifixion from a child's point of view. Children are always interested in other children. Therefore this crucifixion dramatisation is told by children of Jesus' era – children who were present on that eventful day. They tell the story in their words from the time when they hear about the imprisonment of their friend Jesus, the man who loved children and who was so kind to them. They follow Jesus on his road to Calvary and give their account of all the happenings on the journey. After each station, the children meditate on how Jesus' suffering is relevant to the lives of all young people.

The first performance of this dramatisation took place in the Church of the Nativity of Our Lord, Beaumont, Dublin, on Good Friday, 1989. It was a marvellous success. The church was packed to capacity. The children were deservedly congratulated on their wonderful performance. Parents and children in the audience agreed that the dramatisation had unfolded the story of the crucifixion in a new and meaningful manner. It was a story for children by children.

Rita Coleman
Dublin, 1990

CAST

Jesus
Pilate
Mary, mother of Jesus
Simon
Veronica
Joseph of Arimathea
4 soldiers
6 Adults (Introductory Narrative)
3 Children (Introductory Narrative)
3/4 Women of Jerusalem
17 Narrators (14 for the Stations,
2 for the Introduction, 1 for the
Resurrection.)

Total: 40 parts.

Note: As there are so many parts available, children can double up roles, e.g. the narrators can also act as children, adults and women of Jerusalem.

In my production, there were 28 children involved because some of the class of 36 were away on holidays over the Easter period. The other children were only too delighted to oblige by accepting more than one role!

STAGE PROPERTIES

Wooden cross.

Crown of twigs and leaves for the head of Jesus.

Veronica's cloth on which is painted the image of Jesus' face (6th Station).

White cloth for Joseph of Arimathea with which he covers the body of Jesus (14th Station).

Swords, whips and shields for the soldiers.

Binding for Jesus' hands (1st Station).

Two hammers (11th Station).

IMPORTANT

Before each narrative, there is a short dramatisation of the scene in question (See Stage Directions). Then all the actors freeze and the narration begins. The congregation then have a vivid picture on which to focus their attention.

COSTUMES

Jesus
Crown of soft twigs and leaves.
Long, white outer robe and belt
(to be removed at 10th Station).
White hand-towel swathed around a pair of white shorts (visible only after the 10th Station, when the outer robe is removed).

Soldiers

Sandals.
Short brown robe, worn to knee length, cut into four-inch strips from thigh to knee level.

Pilate
Laurel of gold leaves worn on the head.
Richly-coloured robe (perhaps purple) worn over a sheet, and a belt around the waist.
Sandals.

Mary
Dark skirt.
Dark long-sleeved top.
Long, black veil.

Women

Long shawl worn on the head.
Long robe (curtain/sheet/table-cloth/bedspread).
Belt around the waist.

Men
Long robe.
Belt around the waist.
Towel around the head, kept in place with a band.

Children

Short robe worn to knee length.
Belt around the waist.
Sandals.
Narrow strips of material criss-crossed around calves of legs.

INTRODUCTORY SONG

Any suitable song or hymn which the children already know.

INTRODUCTORY NARRATIVE

Stage Directions

From Stage Left: Three adults enter, stand in conversation at centre stage, with their backs to the congregation.

From Stage Right: Three adults enter, stand at stage right in conversation, with their backs to the congregation.

As the first narrator begins, three children enter from stage left. They chat and play together, oblivious of the adults who are in conversation behind them.

At the appropriate part of the narrative, the children notice the adults whispering to each other. The children gesticulate questioningly to one another. They creep over to them and crouch down on all fours to eavesdrop on their conversation. They look suitably saddened and shocked at what they hear, and stay listening to the adults until the end of this introductory piece. Then they stand up, determined to help their friend Jesus, and rush off to find him.

(Narrators)

It was a Friday morning, just like any other Friday in Jerusalem. Early in the morning my friends and I were going to the market to buy food for our mothers. We were having great fun, laughing and joking, talking about school and about Teacher.

Friday is usually busy, but this Friday seemed different. There were many more people than usual around and all the adults were huddled in groups, whispering and talking and arguing. We got close to one group of men to try to find out what all the fuss was about. We heard them say that there had been an arrest in the town the night before and that the trial was to be held that day. We wondered who had been arrested, and crept closer to listen.

Children creep towards adults and crouch on all fours behind them.

We were so sad to hear that it was Jesus, the new teacher from Nazareth, who was under arrest. How could they have arrested him? All the children in our town loved Jesus so much, because he was so kind to us. He was the kindest and most gentle person we had ever met. He often told us lovely stories. He always had time for us; time to listen to our news and to our stories.

But we also knew that many people in Jerusalem hated Jesus, because they saw that Jesus showed love to everyone. They had heard that he made sad people happy, made sick people well, made bad people good, and even made dead people alive again. They were afraid that if Jesus became powerful, they would lose their power and their big jobs.

We discovered that some people in our town planned to get rid of Jesus. He was now under arrest and they were going to make up bad stories about him to tell Pilate, the Roman Governor. If Pilate believed those stories, he could sentence Jesus, our friend, to be killed.

We were so upset. Some of us started to cry, but we decided we would go to Pilate's palace to see if we could do anything for Jesus.

THE FIRST STATION

Stage Directions

Two soldiers roughly push Jesus ahead of them from stage left. Jesus's hands are bound and his head is bowed. The soldiers stand on either side of him. All three stand at centre stage.

Then Pilate enters confidently and stands before Jesus. Pilate looks angry and points to Jesus and then points towards stage left.

The First Station: Jesus is condemned to death.

There is Jesus now, standing quietly and calmly before Pilate. He is bruised and bleeding from beatings. They have made a crown of thorns and put it on his head. Pilate wants to please the people so he believes their false stories about Jesus. He orders that Jesus be crucified.

Oh, poor Jesus, how can they do this to you, you who are so gentle and kind to us all? But how can you be so calm and so quiet when they spread untrue stories about you? Why do you not shout out, 'No, I'm innocent. Stop hurting me!'?

Dear Jesus,
please help me
never to make fun of anyone
or to call people names.
Make me kind and loving to all.

THE SECOND STATION

Stage Directions

Pilate exits stage right. The soldiers carry in a large wooden cross. They give it to Jesus who holds it, with his head bowed. He walks a few steps towards stage left. The soldiers stand towards the back of the stage keeping guard. The men, women and children follow, weeping.

All freeze.

The Second Station: Jesus takes up his cross.

Now the soldiers make Jesus carry a big, heavy cross through the streets. The cross looks so big and heavy and Jesus looks so tired and weak.

Each one of us has our cross to carry; we each have our problems, big and small.

Dear Jesus,
help me to carry my cross.
Help me to study hard in school,
to do my homework well,
and to be helpful and good
for my Mammy and Daddy and Teacher.

THE THIRD STATION

Stage Directions

Jesus walks a few more steps towards stage left and falls to the ground. All the onlookers are horrified. The soldiers show their annoyance. Jesus remains on the ground.

All freeze.

The Third Station: Jesus falls the first time.

Oh no! The cross is too heavy for Jesus – he has fallen to the ground. But look!

Jesus drags himself to his feet and freezes.

He is dragging himself to his feet again and continuing on his way.

Dear Jesus,
help me to be patient with everyone.
When my own cross gets heavy,
help me not to give up easily,
but to struggle on.

THE FOURTH STATION

Stage Directions

Jesus walks slowly a few steps towards centre stage. A woman from the back, Mary, pushes her way to the front and rushes forward towards Jesus with her arms outstretched. Jesus stretches out a hand to her. Mary is crying.

All freeze

The Fourth Station: Jesus meets his mother.

Now Mary, Jesus' mother, pushes herself to the front of the crowd and meets her son, Jesus. How can she cope, knowing that her son is in such pain and will soon have a terrible death?

Oh Jesus,
help us always
to be a comfort to our own mothers,
as you comforted your mother
on that Friday.
They love us so much
and their thoughts and prayers
are always for their children.

THE FIFTH STATION

Stage Directions

The soldiers push Mary back into the crowd which is following Jesus. Jesus walks slowly on but looks very weak and tired. The cross is so heavy.

The soldiers point to the cross and grab a man from the crowd, Simon. Simon shakes his head and protests, but is forced to help Jesus. He lifts the end of Jesus's cross.

All freeze.

The Fifth Station: Simon helps Jesus to carry his cross.

The soldiers notice that Jesus is too exhausted to go on, so they force a man called Simon to help Jesus to carry his cross.

Oh Jesus,
help me always to be willing
to help others who are in need.
I do not want to be selfish;
help me to show love and compassion
to everyone.

THE SIXTH STATION

The Sixth Station: Veronica wipes the face of Jesus.

Look! I see our neighbour, Veronica, wiping the face of Jesus with a cloth. His kind, loving face is covered with sweat and blood. Where did she get the courage to rush past the soldiers and act in such a kind manner?

The soldiers are very angry with her, but Jesus smiles and thanks her.

The image of his face stays on that cloth as a reminder of all that Jesus suffered today.

Dear Jesus,
help me to be kind like Veronica.
Teach me to show love and kindness
to others always.

SEVENTH STATION

Jesus walks on wearily, to stage right, then falls again to the ground. The soldiers gesticulate angrily.

The Seventh Station: Jesus falls the second time.

Jesus is so tired that he falls again under the weight of the heavy cross. He is bruised and bleeding and the soldiers whip him to hurry him along.

Dear Jesus,
help me to be strong and determined
when nothing seems to be going right
for me.
When I am not doing well in school,
help me to keep on trying
and to do my best to improve.
Please don't let me give up.

EIGHTH STATION

Stage Directions

Jesus drags himself to his feet and moves on slowly. At stage right, three women come forward to speak to him. They are crying and stretch out their hands towards him. Jesus stretches out a weary hand to them.

All freeze.

The Eighth Station: Jesus speaks to the women of Jerusalem.

I see my mother and some of the other women crying and feeling so sorry for Jesus. They love him very much. As he passes them, Jesus speaks to them, even though he is very tired and weak. He asks them not to cry for him and they seem to be comforted by his words.

Dear Jesus,
help me to be a comfort to others
when they are suffering.
Teach me not to think of my own troubles,
but to reach out
and help my family and friends.

NINTH STATION

Stage Directions

The women return to the crowd. Jesus struggles towards the centre stage. The onlookers remain at stage right. Jesus falls again. The soldiers are beside him.

All freeze.

The Ninth Station: Jesus falls the third time.

By now, Jesus is absolutely exhausted. He has come to the hill where he will be crucified and, as he carries the cross up the hill, he falls the third time. I'm sure he feels that he can't go on any more.

Dear Jesus,
give me the courage and strength
to go on when I am not doing well
in school or at home.

TENTH STATION

Stage Directions

The soldiers drag Jesus to his feet. He stands before them with his head bowed as they tear off his outer robe. They throw this aside.

All freeze.

The Tenth Station: Jesus is stripped of his clothes.

The soldiers now roughly tear Jesus' clothes from his battered, blood-stained body. He looks so weak and frail.

Poor Jesus,
they have taken away your clothes,
but they have not taken away
your great love for us.
You have shown love to us
when we abandoned you.
Help us never to abandon you again,
but to love you always.

ELEVENTH STATION

The soldiers place the cross on the ground with the foot facing the congregation. Two soldiers take Jesus by the arms and lay him on the cross on the ground. The third soldier brings the hammers to them. They then begin to hammer loudly on the arms of the cross. Jesus' feet jerk with pain.

As the narrative continues, the soldiers mime the actions of hammering.

 The Eleventh Station: Jesus is nailed to the cross

Oh, the agony Jesus is in as the soldiers nail his hands and feet to the big, heavy cross. I cannot bear to look at the pain on Jesus' face. But still, he asks his Father in heaven to forgive the soldiers. Is there no end to this man's compassion and love and forgiveness?

Dear Jesus,
help me to love and forgive
my family and friends,
even when they hurt me.
Teach me not to bear grudges
and have enemies,
but to forgive and forget.

TWELFTH STATION

Stage Directions

One soldier holds the foot of the cross from the front and the other two raise up the cross by the two arms. Jesus is raised up with it, and stands with his arms outstretched on the cross. Two soldiers stand on either side and one soldier crouches behind the cross, giving it support. Mary and John come from the crowd and kneel on either side of the cross.

All freeze.

At the appropriate moment in the narrative, Jesus bows his head and dies.

The Twelfth Station: Jesus dies on the cross.

After three long hours on the cross, poor Jesus dies. Darkness settles over the land, even though it is only three o'clock in the afternoon. The earth trembles and we are all afraid. I am so sad to see Jesus dead on the cross.

Dear Jesus,
I know you have died on the cross today
to show me how much you love me.
There is no end to your love.
You died to save me.
I do not deserve all this love
and yet I know
that you will love me always.

THIRTEENTH STATION

Stage Directions

*Two men from the crowd go to the cross
and take down the limp body of Jesus.
Mary, still kneeling, holds out her arms for
the body, which is then placed in her arms.
John goes to comfort Mary and puts his
arm around her. Mary bows her head in
grief. The soldier who is supporting the
cross, from his crouched rear position, remains there with the cross.*

The Thirteenth Station:
Jesus is taken down from the cross.

The body of Jesus is taken down from the cross. His
heart-broken mother, Mary, holds him in her arms and
cries. It is so sad to watch her holding the limp body of
her son.

Dear Jesus,
help me to be a comfort to others
when they are sad.
Help me to console my mother
and my friends
when they are upset.

FOURTEENTH STATION

Stage Directions

Joseph, from Arimathea, enters from stage right, carrying a large, white sheet. He shows the sheet to Mary and then uses it to cover the body of Jesus. Then he and three other men carry the body of Jesus to the tomb, at the back of centre stage. A soldier stands guard before the tomb. Everyone is weeping.

All freeze.

The Fourteenth Station: Jesus is laid in the tomb.

A kind neighbour called Joseph offers a tomb to Mary for the body of Jesus. With great love and sadness, his body is wrapped in a clean sheet and laid in the tomb. His tomb is in a small garden. A big stone blocks the opening of the tomb. A soldier is ordered to stand guard over the tomb in case somebody steals the body of Jesus.

HYMN AND PROCESSION

All the children sing:
Were you there when they crucified my Lord?

Verse 1: Were you there when they crucified my Lord?
Verse 2: Were you there when they nailed him to a tree?
Verse 3: Were you there when they laid him in the tomb?

Stage Directions

When the song begins, the mourners will file in lonely, sad procession, around the church. Mary will lead the mourners in the procession.

Mary, with John's comforting arm around her, slowly begins to walk towards stage right and down the side isle of the church. Simon, Veronica, the men, women, narrators and all the mourners slowly make their way right round the church, singing 'Were you there when they crucified my Lord?'

Now the stage is empty, except for the poignant sight of the cross, which is supported at the rear by a hidden soldier. A soldier stands guard outside the tomb.

The procession continues around the church and the Our Father, Hail Mary and Glory be are said until the procession reaches the altar again.

As the children file back to the altar steps, they kneel, one after the other, on the bottom step of the altar.

When all have knelt, the final narrative commences.

FINAL NARRATIVE

Stage Directions

When the children hear that Jesus is alive again, their faces light up with joy and they talk to one another excitedly.

Jesus throws away his covering and stands up. The soldier who is on guard sees him and throws down his shield and sword in terror. He flees from the altar, down the middle aisle of the church and out of sight.

Jesus, slowly and with his hands joined, walks from the altar and down the centre aisle of the church. After a pause, the children walk slowly and happily after him, led first by Mary and John. Joyfully, they sing an Alleluia song.

The altar is left with the upright cross as a reminder of the events of that weekend.

The children proceed round the church and return to the altar, singing their Alleluia.

But later on we were to discover that this was not the end of the story of Jesus, but the beginning of his story.

On Sunday morning, when friends went to his tomb to pray, they found it empty. The stone had been rolled away and an angel told them that Jesus was no longer dead, but that he was alive again! They could not believe the news. Jesus was dead and now he is alive again! They were so happy, and so were we!

CONCLUDING HYMN

An Alleluia hymn.